INSANE, WACKY WORLD!

ROAR!

EXTREME CAR FACTS

by E. C. Andrews

BEARPORT PUBLISHING

Minneapolis, Minnesota

Credits
Images are courtesy of Shutterstock.com. With thanks to Getty Images, Thinkstock Photo, and iStockphoto. Cover – Adrien The, Olha Kostiuk, art-sonik, Victor Metelskiy, Alena Nv, hvostik, Pogorelova Olga, KingVector, Irina Adamovich. 4–5 – Mikbiz, Perfect_kebab, Brandon Woyshnis, Aleksandr Artt, SpicyTruffel. 6–7 – Daria Pushka, FernandoV. 8–9 – GEORGE STAMATIS, Pikovit, Claire, Slingerland, Nutkins.J. 10–11 – Andrii Lysenko, kateetc, I Pokotylo, johavel, Iurii Davydov, Karuna Tansuk, Alfmaler, VikiVector. 12–13 – lennystan, Nikita Anokhin, Polina MB, Gercen. 14–15 – Sopotnicki, WladD, GalinaBahlyk, Smarta, Svvell Design. 16–17 – asharkyu, Net Vector, betto rodrigues, 32 pixels. 18–19 – Blulz60, Boykov, HappyPictures, Double Brain, maryartist. 20–21 – Rodrigo Garrido, Ronn Hook, Fayzulin Serg, Avigator Fortuner, Denissenko Oleg. 22–23 – TaurusEmerald, Mechanik, Maksim Shmeljov, Nigel Jarvis, Double Brain. 24–25 – Gestalt Imagery, Erica Finstad, vector arts and creative. 26–27 – Matthew Troke, VIAVAL TOURS, Mor65_Mauro Piccardi, Net Vector. 28–29 – Phonlamai Photo, Pavel Chagochkin, yokunen. 30–31 – PBabic, summersetretrievers.

Bearport Publishing Company Product Development Team
President: Jen Jenson; Director of Product Development: Spencer Brinker; Managing Editor: Allison Juda; Associate Editor: Naomi Reich; Associate Editor: Tiana Tran; Art Director: Colin O'Dea; Designer: Kim Jones; Designer: Kayla Eggert; Product Development Assistant: Owen Hamlin

Library of Congress Cataloging-in-Publication Data is available at www.loc.gov or upon request from the publisher.

ISBN: 979-8-89232-066-5 (hardcover)
ISBN: 979-8-89232-540-0 (paperback)
ISBN: 979-8-89232-199-0 (ebook)

For more information, write to Bearport Publishing, 5357 Penn Avenue South, Minneapolis, MN 55419.

CONTENTS

INSANE, WACKY CARS

Cars help get us from place to place. But there is so much more to cars than just pressing down on a gas pedal and cruising forward.

There are many different kinds of cars. From flying cars to cars that can run on cheese, each one is **extreme** in its own way.

CARS THAT RUN ON CHEESE ARE NACHO AVERAGE CAR!

Let's learn about some insane, wacky cars!

THE FIRST CARS

In 1478, Leonardo da Vinci was the first person to **design** a car. But Leonardo never built his moving machine. . . .

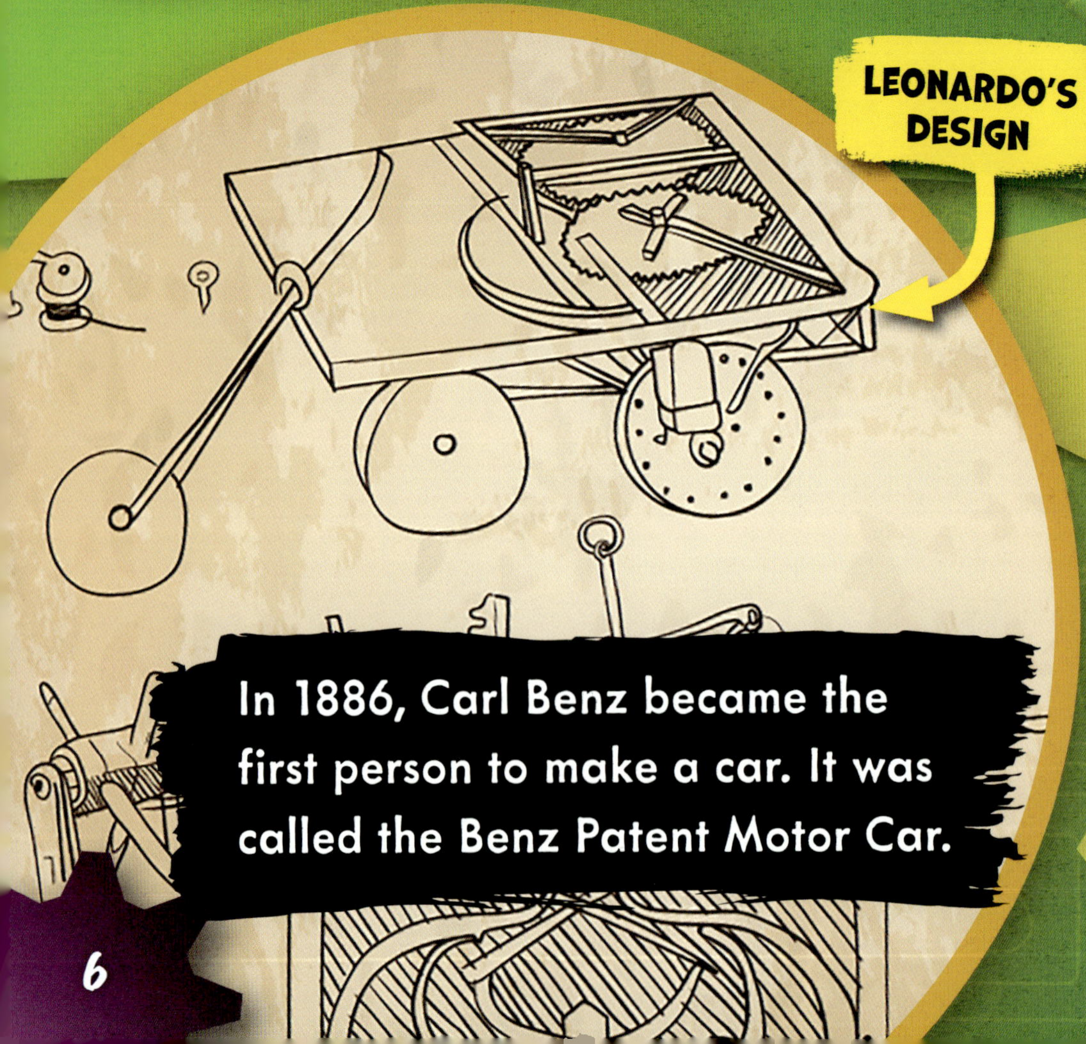

In 1886, Carl Benz became the first person to make a car. It was called the Benz Patent Motor Car.

Carl's wife Bertha took the first long-distance journey in a car in 1888. She drove the car for 12 hours and went about 60 miles (100 km)!

THE BENZ PATENT MOTOR CAR

WINDUP CARS

Back in the day, most cars were wound up with a crank handle. But people had to be very careful.

LOTS OF PEOPLE BROKE THEIR WRISTS ON THESE HANDLES!

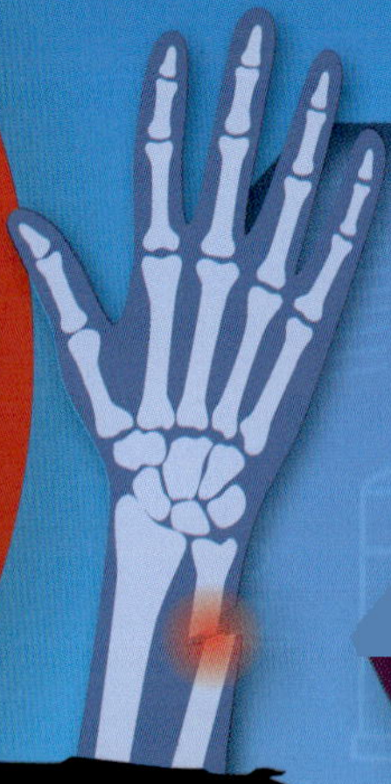

Sometimes, the handle would fly off and hit people in the face. Other times, the engine would start very suddenly and move the handle.

Today, we still use a tiny version of the crank handle on windup toys. A woman in California has the largest collection of these toys. She has 1,258 of them!

The most windup toy cars set off at the same time is 286. Watch out!

FANCY FUELS

King Charles III of England owns a car that mostly runs on white wine and whey. Whey is something left over from making cheese.

THIS IS WHEY? NO WAY!

King Charles III's car isn't the only one that runs on strange things. Some cars use wood or coffee as **fuel**. Others even run on the fat left over from cooking french fries!

WEIRD WHEELS

There are many cars with weird wheels. While most cars have four, there are some that have more . . . or fewer!

Some Formula 1 race cars have six wheels. The fastest vehicle with one wheel can reach speeds up to 80 mph (130 kph).

Some tanks and trucks have tracks over their wheels to help them move across uneven or icy ground.

THERE'S NO DE-FEET WITH THIS CAR!

One three-wheeled car is shaped like a giant shoe.

FROM MASSIVE TO MINI

The American Dream is the longest stretch limousine in the world. It has 26 wheels.

IT CAN FIT 75 PEOPLE INSIDE!

This limousine comes with a waterbed, a swimming pool, a diving board, and a mini-golf course.

While the American Dream may be **massive**, some cars are absolutely mini! The Peel P50 is the smallest car ever made.

This mini car is 5 feet (1 m) long and has only three wheels.

PRINTED CARS

The way we make cars has changed. Today, we can use 3D printers to make whole cars.

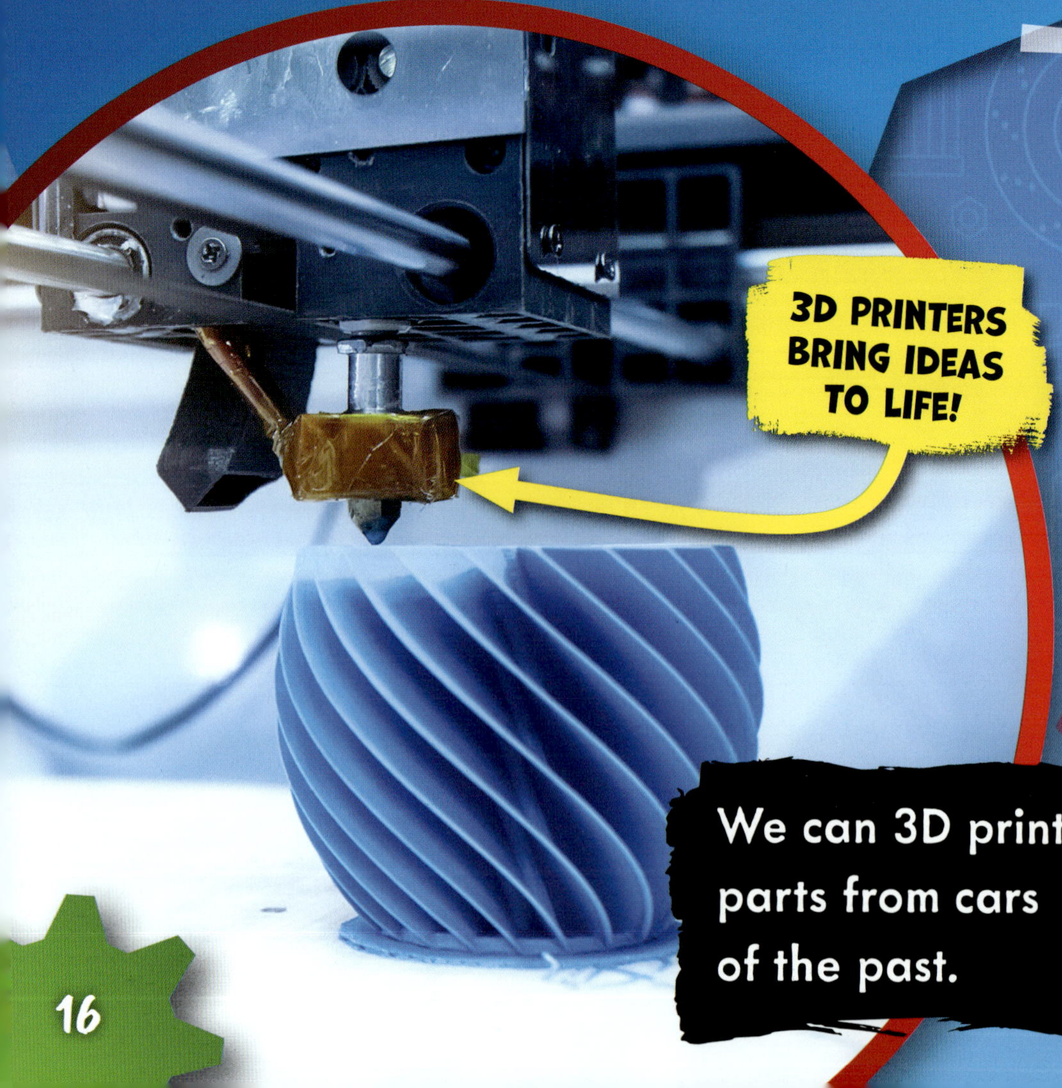

3D PRINTERS BRING IDEAS TO LIFE!

We can 3D print parts from cars of the past.

3D printers can also create modern cars. People have made a 3D printed high-tech supercar.

This supercar can go from 0 to 60 mph (100 kph) in 2 seconds. *Zoom!*

EXTREME CAR RACES

Car races are extreme, but some are crazy and extreme.

A SOAP BOX DERBY CAR

The Soap Box Derby is a race with cars made out of things such as wood and plastic. These cars rely on **gravity** to pull them downhill.

Racers in Florida like to challenge one another to races taking heavy school buses around a racetrack.

Not all races are just about going fast. Some last a long time, too. During **endurance** races, teams of drivers take turns racing for 24 hours straight!

SUPER STUNTS

A SIDE WHEELIE IS DRIVING ON ONLY TWO WHEELS!

The fastest car side wheelie was done at 115 mph (185 kph).

The longest jump in a car made it 330 ft. (100 m).

When drivers turn quickly while driving fast, their cars skid sideways. This is called drifting. In 2016, the record was set for the fastest drift at 190 mph (305 kph).

The longest drift traveled 232 miles (374 km).

MEGA MONSTER TRUCKS

The largest monster truck in the world is called Bigfoot 5.

The giant truck is 15 ft. (5 m) tall. Its tires alone are 10 ft. (3 m) tall.

The longest monster truck is called the Sin City Hustler. It is 32 ft. (10 m) long.

THE MOHAWK WARRIOR WAS SPONSORED BY A HAIR SALON.

The fastest a monster truck has gone is 102 mph (164 kph).

THE FABULOUS HUDSON HORNET

Some of the most famous race cars were Fabulous Hudson Hornets.

Hudson Hornet race cars were made in the early 1950s. They soon took on a new racing name and became some of the best **NASCAR** race cars in the United States.

Between 1951 and 1955, the newly named Fabulous Hudson Hornet race cars won 79 races and 3 championships.

In 1952, they won 27 of the 34 NASCAR races they took part in.

AMPHIBIOUS CARS

Some extreme cars can drive across water as well as land. These are called **amphibious** (am-FIB-ee-uhs) cars.

DON'T OPEN THE DOORS!

Amphibious cars were first built in Germany in 1961. Later, they became very popular in the United States.

The Amphicar is one of the first amphibious cars ever made. But only 3,878 of them were built.

In 2008, another amphibious car set the speed record for crossing the English Channel. It took 1 hour and 14 minutes.

FLYING CARS

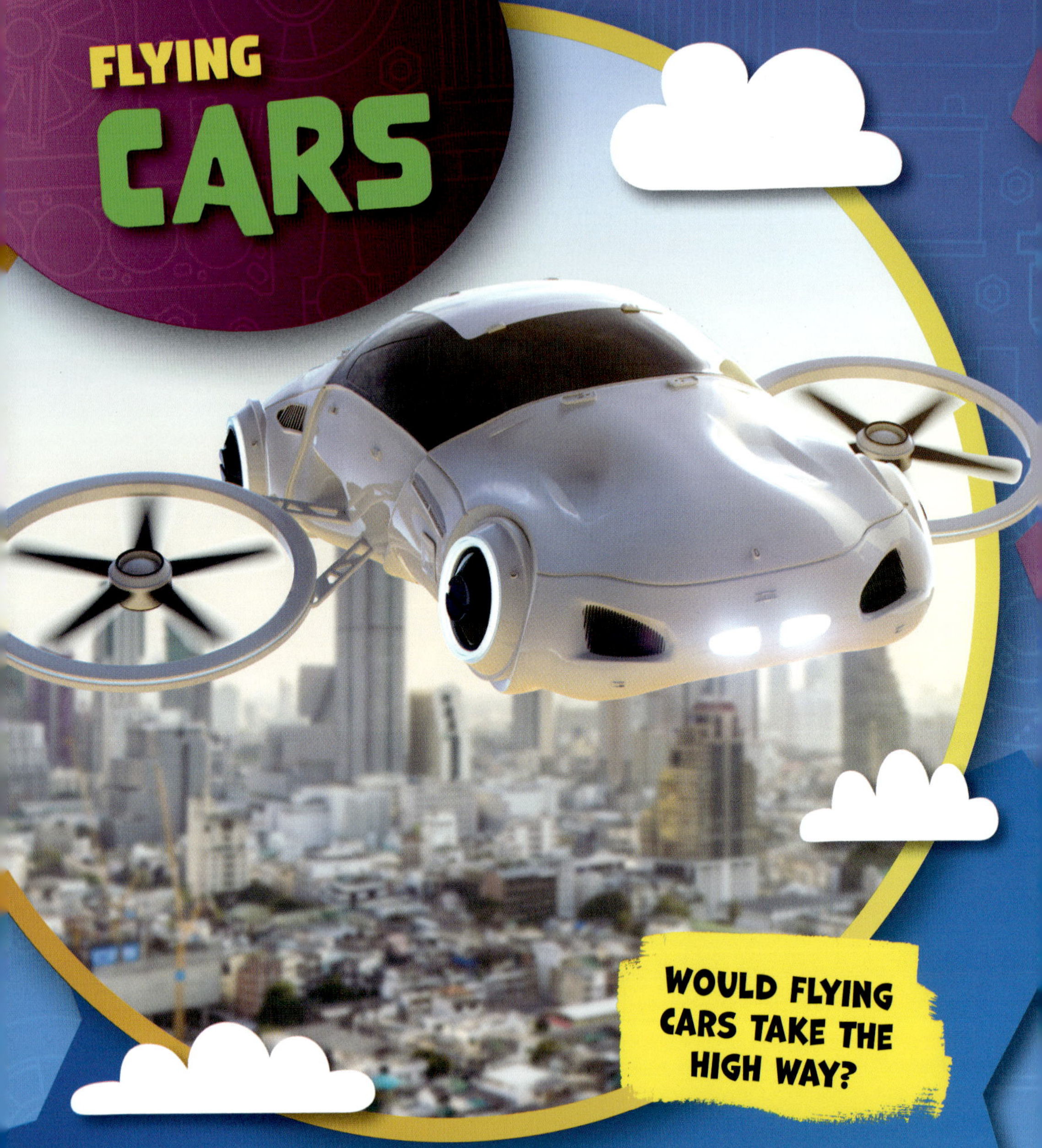

WOULD FLYING CARS TAKE THE HIGH WAY?

Water cars are one thing, but what about flying cars? In 1917, Glenn Curtiss built a flying car, but it never took to the skies.

Scientists are working on flying cars. The Transition is a plane that can fold its wings away to become a normal car on the road!

Today, many people are designing flying cars. You just might be able to see one in the next few years!

SUPER CRAZY CARS

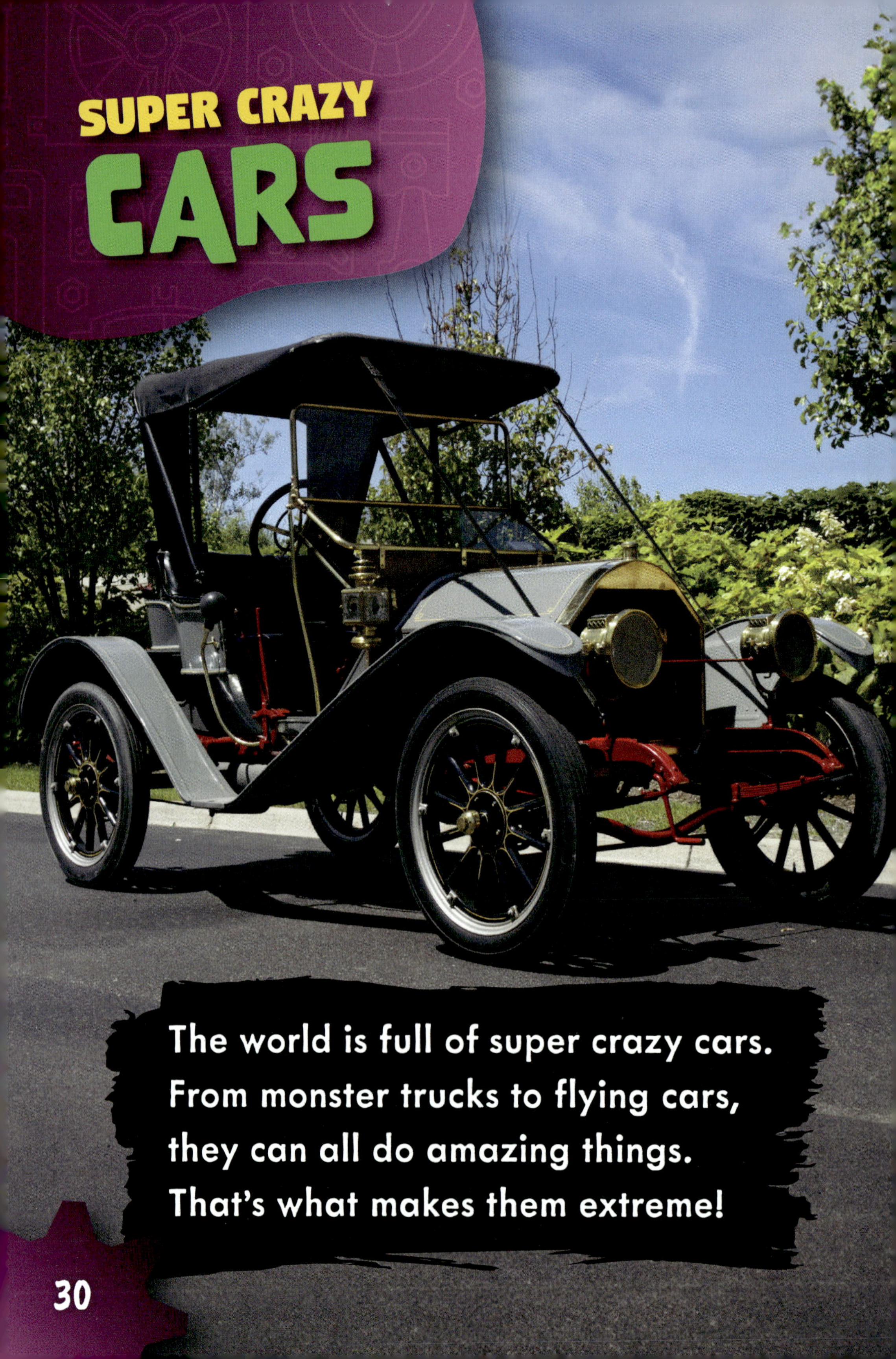

The world is full of super crazy cars. From monster trucks to flying cars, they can all do amazing things. That's what makes them extreme!

GLOSSARY

amphibious able to be used on land and in the water

design to draw and plan how something will look and work

endurance the ability to keep going

extreme at the highest level with an element of risk

fuel to give energy or power to something

gravity the invisible force that pulls everything toward Earth

massive large

NASCAR a type of stock car racing that includes racing down a track

sponsored funded by a company

INDEX

READ MORE

Bylenga, Heather Rook. *NASCAR Racing (Racing Sports).* Mendota Heights, MN: Apex, 2024.

Flynn, Heather Rook. *Car Racing Records Smashed! (Sports Illustrated Kids. Record Smashers).* North Mankato, MN: Capstone Press, 2024.

LEARN MORE ONLINE

1. Go to **www.factsurfer.com** or scan the QR code below.
2. Enter "**Car Facts**" into the search box.
3. Click on the cover of this book to see a list of websites.